Do you have a favorite holiday? Some people like the Fourth of July best. Many kids march in parades.

1

People from India say hello to
the new year by lighting candles.

They wear flowers, too. The flowers are pink, red, purple, or white.

The Chinese welcome their
new year with a parade. Some
people dress up as dragons or
other animals. They set off
firecrackers for luck.

At night, thousands of lanterns fill the streets for the Festival of Lanterns.

Kids in one place in New Mexico dress up like people who lived a long time ago. They are proud of who they are.

These kids are from Mexico.
In Mexico, May fifth is a holiday.
Lots of people dance on Cinco de
Mayo.

These Native Americans do an old dance at their festival.

It is called the Corn Dance.
The dancers ask for rain to help
the corn grow.

Earth Day is a special day in
many parts of the world. People
take care of the earth on this day.

People plant trees. They clean up litter. They do what they can to help.

Halloween is an American holiday. Children wear costumes and eat candy.

People carve pumpkins. They
tell scary stories about bats and
ghosts.

There are many ways to enjoy holidays. Some people have contests. Some people cheer and shout.

Some people wear special clothes. Some people play outside.

We all like holidays. Holidays bring us together.

What is your favorite holiday?